LEADER GUIDE

FORGIVEN
THE TRANSFORMING POWER OF CONFESSION

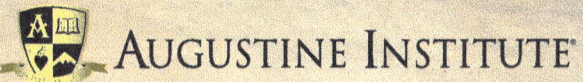
AUGUSTINE INSTITUTE

FORGIVEN™
THE TRANSFORMING POWER OF CONFESSION

Nihil Obstat: Fr. Gary B. Selin, S. T. D., *Censor Deputatus*
Imprimatur: Most Reverend Samuel J. Aquila, S.T.L., Archbishop of Denver
October 5, 2017

Copyright © 2016 Augustine Institute. All rights reserved.
With the exception of short excerpts used in articles and critical reviews, no part of this work may be reproduced, transmitted, or stored in any form whatsoever, printed or electronic, without the prior permission of the publisher.

Some Scripture verses contained herein are from the New Testament, copyright 1946; Old Testament, copyright 1952; The Apocrypha, copyright 1957; Revised Standard Version Bible, Catholic Edition, Copyright © 1965, 1966, Division of Christian Education of the National Council of the Churches of Christ in the United States of America; Revised Standard Version Bible, Ignatius Edition, Copyright © 2006, Division of Christian Education of the National Council of the Churches of Christ in the United States of America.

English translation of the *Catechism of the Catholic Church* for the United States of America, copyright ©1994, United States Catholic Conference, Inc.—Libreria Editrice Vaticana. English translation of the *Catechism of the Catholic Church:* Modification from the Editio Typica copyright ©1997, United States Catholic Conference, Inc.—Libreria Editrice Vaticana.

Writers: Ashley Crane, Lucas Pollice, Sean Dalton, Becca Arend
Print Production/Graphic Design: Jeff Cole, Brenda Kraft, Christina Gray, Devin Schadt, Kathleen McCarty, Ann Diaz
Media: Steve Flanigan, Aurora Cerulli, Jon Ervin, Matthew Krekeler, Justin Leddick, Kevin Mallory, Ted Mast, Edward Sri, Molly Sweeney

AUGUSTINE INSTITUTE

6160 South Syracuse Way, Suite 310
Greenwood Village, CO 80111
Information: 303-937-4420
formed.org

Printed in the United States of America
ISBN 978-0-9972037-7-6

TABLE OF CONTENTS

OVERVIEW & PROGRAM 2-10

SESSION 1:
Where Are You? 13-21

SESSION 2:
An Encounter with Mercy 23-33

SESSION 3:
The Rite Explained 35-47

SESSION 4:
Biblical Foundations: Sin, Mercy, and the Sacrament of Confession 49-59

SESSION 5:
Answering Common Questions about Confession 61-71

Forgiven: AN OVERVIEW

Welcome to the FORGIVEN™ program. These sessions have been carefully designed to help Catholics more deeply encounter the great gift of God's mercy in the Sacrament of Penance and Reconciliation and to help this sacrament become a regular part of their spiritual journey. FORGIVEN has also been designed in a particular way to help parents prepare for their child's First Confession. This series will explore the profound effects and healing grace of the Sacrament of Reconciliation.

In this series, the participants will discover the merciful way that God seeks us out when we have sinned and calls us back to himself. They will examine the sacrament from the perspective of both the priest and the penitent, and they will explore the scriptural foundation of the sacrament. This study will help them recognize the beauty of the Rite of Penance and the transformative power of the grace God offers us in this sacrament.

The FORGIVEN series utilizes three components—this Leader Guide, the Study Guide for participants, and session videos—to communicate its message. All three are designed to complement one another to educate participants and encourage parents.

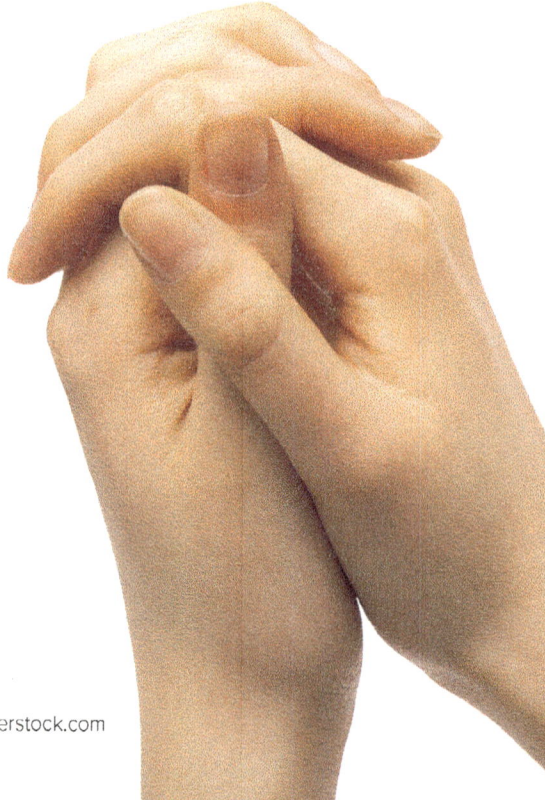

Woman clasps hands © TongRo Images Inc. / shutterstock.com

How the FORGIVEN Program Works

The FORGIVEN program is comprised of the following five sessions (plus a bonus video for children):

- **Where Are You?** examines our experience of guilt and how God seeks us out and calls us back to himself after we have sinned.

- **An Encounter with Mercy** focuses on the incredible mercy that God offers us in the Sacrament of Reconciliation.

- **The Rite Explained** looks at the sacrament from the perspective of the priest and walks through each step of the rite as well as how to make an examination of conscience in preparation for Confession.

- **Biblical Foundations: Sin, Mercy, and the Sacrament of Confession** explores God's revelation of his merciful love in Scripture and how this pattern of our loving Father forgiving the sins of his children provides the foundation for the sacrament.

- **Answering Common Questions about Confession** addresses some of the most frequently asked questions about the sacrament, including why we need to confess our sins to a priest, what actually happens during Confession, and how speaking about our sins and receiving reconciliation heals us.

- **For Children: How to Make a Good Confession** is an engaging and encouraging walk through the sacrament. This bonus video shows children what they will see, hear, and do when making their First Confession. It covers the examination of conscience, what the confessional looks like, each step of the Rite of Penance, and what is penance.

The FORGIVEN series can be completed over the course of five separate meetings or during a day-long seminar. FORGIVEN would also be an ideal resource for an Advent or Lenten parish study, or even for a parish mission.

Sacramental Preparation Sessions for Parents

For the formation of parents for their children's First Confession, we recommend the first three sessions, which can be conducted separately or in one longer session. The Parish Edition also includes a Bonus Session for parents, which can be used in these parent sessions. See the end of this Introduction for ideas on how to schedule parent sessions.

LEADING A FORGIVEN SESSION

The Leader Guide

This guide takes the leader through the step-by-step process for each session. The various sections are carefully crafted to equip the leader to lead participants through an opening of their hearts and minds to God's Word and the teachings of the Catholic Church regarding Confession.

What You'll Find in Each FORGIVEN Session

SESSION OVERVIEW: An overview of the session gives the leader a simple summary of the content that will be presented and provides context for the topic.

SESSION OBJECTIVES: The objectives clearly describe what the participants should take away from each session.

STEP 1: OPENING PRAYER and INTRODUCTION: The Prayer and Introduction are included in both the Leader Guide and the Study Guide. Invite participants to pray along silently or aloud. Then read the Introduction.

STEP 2: CONNECT: Each session begins with questions that help participants get to know one another on a deeper level.

STEP 3: VIDEO: The video segment teaches the subject using Sacred Scripture and Sacred Tradition of the Catholic Church and by sharing stories and testimonials. The Leader Guide and Study Guide both include a brief outline that follows the key points in the teaching.

STEP 4: DISCUSS: These questions help participants reflect on the topics of the session together. If you have a large group, consider forming smaller groups for the discussion, with team members facilitating and keeping each small group on track.

We have included possible responses for the Small Group Discussion questions in this Leader Guide. Use these to help get a discussion started, bring greater clarity to the study topic, or answer a difficult question.

STEP 5: COMMIT—ENCOUNTERING GOD'S MERCY: This not only calls the participants to more fully understand the Sacrament of Reconciliation, but also invites them to a deeper conversion to Christ and his Church. Preview this briefly with participants.

STEP 6: WRAP-UP AND CLOSING PRAYER: The wrap-up summarizes the key points of the session. The prayer is included in both the Leader Guide and the Study Guide. Invite participants to read along silently or aloud.

DIGGING DEEPER: Both the Leader Guide and the Study Guide include quotations by the saints and excerpts from the *Catechism of the Catholic Church* and other Catholic works to help further the participants' understanding of a particular topic.

FOR FURTHER STUDY: Each session concludes with suggested resources for continued study and reflection, which may be of interest to participants, parents, and leaders.

The Study Guide

The Study Guide contains all the information a participant will need to fruitfully participate. Each session includes a brief Introduction, the Opening Prayer, an outline of the Video, the Small Group Discussion questions, Digging Deeper quotes, the Commit reflection, and the Closing Prayer. Each person should have his or her own Study Guide.

HOW TO LEAD SMALL GROUPS

The success of any small group begins with an engaged leader. Leading a small group discussion does not mean you have to lecture or teach. A successful small group leader facilitates, getting group participants to interact with each other as they make new discoveries. Here are some tips to help you get started as you lead and facilitate your small group:

- **Set the Tone:** Let group members know from the beginning that your time together is meant to be for discussion and discovery, not lecture. Also remind participants that every question and answer is welcomed and worthy of discussion.

- **Encourage Involvement:** Work to invite all participants to engage in discussion. Don't be afraid of periods of silence, especially during the first part of the meeting. If one person gets off track, kindly acknowledge the person and invite him or her to explore that topic more after your group time. Ask questions such as "What do the rest of you think?" or "Anyone else?" to encourage several people to respond.

- **Open-Ended Questions:** Use questions that invite thought-provoking answers rather than "yes" or "no," "true" or "false," or a one-word, fill-in-the-blank answer. As a leader, your job is to get participants to think about the topic and how the Scriptures and reflections can be relevant and applicable to their own life of faith.

- **Affirm Answers:** People are often reluctant to speak up for fear of saying something wrong or giving an incorrect answer. Affirm every participant by saying things such as "Great idea," "I hadn't thought of that before," or "That's an insightful response." These types of phrases communicate that you value everyone's comments and opinions.

- **Avoid Advice:** Remember, you're acting as a facilitator—not a college professor or counselor. Instead of giving advice or lecturing, when appropriate, offer how a Scripture passage or something in the video spoke to you personally, or give an example of how you've been able to apply a specific concept in your own life.

- **Be Flexible and Real:** Sometimes your group time may veer off-track due to something that's going on in our culture or your community (which sometimes leads to public apologies for sinful behavior). Use relevant topics as a time to remind participants that God is always with us and that we can seek guidance from Scripture, from the Church's teachings, and from the Holy Spirit in every situation. If you model relevant discussion and transparency, your group participants are more likely to do the same.

- **Stick around after the Meeting:** As the leader, make yourself available after your meeting time for questions, concerns, or further discussion on a topic that a participant may have been hesitant about during the scheduled time. If a question arises that has you stumped, admit that you don't have the answer and offer to contact someone who may be able to provide one, such as your parish priest or deacon, or your diocese.

FIVE-SEPARATE-MEETINGS OPTION

Below is the suggested outline for an individual session when using FORGIVEN **over five separate 90-minute meetings.**

Use the time allotments as a guideline; the length of time spent on each section will vary from group to group.

TIME	STEPS	OVERVIEW
5 Minutes	OPENING PRAYER/ INTRODUCTION	Welcome everyone, share the Opening Prayer, and then go through the Introduction of the session.
10 Minutes	CONNECT	Ask the Connect questions to get participants acquainted with the topic.
30 Minutes	VIDEO	Watch the video segment together.
20 Minutes	DISCUSS	Facilitate discussion of the questions in small groups.
10 Minutes	BREAK	
10 Minutes	COMMIT	Lead participants in a brief overview of the Commit take-home assignment.
5 Minutes	WRAP-UP AND CLOSING PRAYER	Review the main points, and finish with the Closing Prayer.

DAY-LONG OPTION

FORGIVEN can also be facilitated in a day-long program with shorter sessions. Here's an example of how you might structure the day:

8:30 a.m.	Registration/Gathering/Introductions
9:00–10:00 a.m.	Session 1
	BREAK
10:15–11:15 a.m.	Session 2
	BREAK
11:30 a.m.–12:30 p.m.	Session 3
	BREAK
1:30–2:30 p.m.	Session 4
	BREAK
2:45–3:45 p.m.	Session 5

For each 60-minute session, use the suggested format below:

TIME	STEPS	OVERVIEW
5 Minutes	OPENING PRAYER/ INTRODUCTION	Welcome everyone, share the Opening Prayer, and then go through the Introduction of the session.
10 Minutes	CONNECT	Ask the Connect questions to get participants acquainted with the topic.
25 Minutes	VIDEO	Watch the video segment together.
10 Minutes	DISCUSS	Facilitate discussion of the questions in small groups.
5 Minutes	COMMIT	Lead participants in a brief overview of the Commit take-home assignment.
5 Minutes	WRAP-UP AND CLOSING PRAYER	Review the main points, and finish with the Closing Prayer.

SACRAMENTAL PREPARATION PARENT MEETING FORMAT

FORGIVEN can be shared with parents in a variety of ways. Here are some ideas:

One Session:

Parishes can conduct a single 2½-hour session parent meeting using the first three sessions of FORGIVEN by having 10 minutes of small group discussion after each episode and two short breaks.

Two Sessions:

Parishes can offer two 2-hour sessions following the 60-minute format above, presenting the sessions as follows:

>   **Session 1:** FORGIVEN Sessions 1 and 2
>   **Session 2:** FORGIVEN Session 3 and Parent Bonus Session*

Three Sessions:

Parishes can also offer three 2-hour sessions following the 60-minute format above and presenting each of the sessions, as follows:

>   **Session 1:** FORGIVEN Sessions 1 and 2
>   **Session 2:** FORGIVEN Sessions 3 and 4
>   **Session 3:** FORGIVEN Session 5 and Parent Bonus Session*

*The Bonus Parent Session does not include a Leader Guide or Study Guide. It is 16 minutes long and can be followed by a small group discussion, asking parents to discuss ways in which they can best prepare their children for their First Confession.

NOTES

NOTES

FORGIVEN™
THE TRANSFORMING POWER OF CONFESSION

SESSION 1
Where Are You?

SESSION 1 | WHERE ARE YOU?

> **SESSION OVERVIEW**

Read this overview in advance to familiarize yourself with the session.

In his letter to the Romans, St. Paul says that **"all have sinned and fall short of the glory of God"** (Romans 3:23). Sin—and the resulting guilt—is a universal experience. Maybe we try to justify our sins and ignore the guilt. Maybe the guilt becomes all-consuming, and we can't see a way out. But that guilt isn't meant to be ignored or to consume us. Guilt is a wake-up call, and God wants to use it to draw us mercifully back to himself.

Our encounter with God in the Sacrament of Reconciliation always begins with God seeking us. The guilt that we experience when we sin is God's merciful call to us, just as he called out to Adam and Eve in the Garden of Eden: **"Where are you?"** (Genesis 3:9). God seeks us out when we have sinned, not to scold or punish us, but to offer us his healing and his forgiveness. It's certainly true that God is omnipotent and just, but before all else he is our loving, merciful Father. If we understand this, then guilt is not something bad to be avoided or ignored, or another wound in our already broken hearts; rather, it becomes a step toward reconciliation.

When we are confronted with feelings of guilt, we have an opportunity: Will we find ways to distract ourselves and justify our behavior, or will we recognize God's wake-up call and make the necessary changes in our lives? God is walking in the garden of our lives, calling to each one of us: "Where are you?" Will you allow him to find you and heal you?

> **DIGGING DEEPER**
> Contrition, which is sorrow for sin, is good because it means that we want to repent and be reconciled to God. There are two types of contrition: (1) perfect, which means that we are sorry because we love God above all else and are sorry that we have offended him (see CCC 1452); and (2) imperfect, which means that we are sorry because we are horrified by the ugliness of our sin and/or we fear the resulting punishment for our sins (see CCC 1453).

While the guilt that results from a conscience properly formed by the moral law can lead us to repentance and reconciliation with God, it is important to point out that some guilt may result from an improperly formed conscience. Likewise, the absence of guilt does not necessarily point to moral uprightness as the precepts of the natural law can be erased from one's conscience. Thus, a proper consideration of guilt should take into consideration conscience and the moral law.

SESSION OBJECTIVES

- Understand that God uses our feelings of guilt to get our attention and to show us that something needs to change.
- Recognize the various ways that we tend to react to an experience of guilt.
- Understand that God is a loving Father who seeks us out when we sin.

STEP 1: OPENING PRAYER

*Begin this session by leading the **OPENING PRAYER**, which is also found in the Study Guide on page 6. Then read or summarize the **INTRODUCTION** for your group.*

Out of the depths I cry to you, O Lord!
Lord, hear my voice!
Let your ears be attentive to the voice
of my supplications!
If you, O Lord, should mark iniquities,
Lord, who could stand?
But there is forgiveness with you,
that you may be feared.
I wait for the Lord, my soul waits,
and in his word I hope;
my soul waits for the Lord
more than watchmen for the morning,
more than watchmen for the morning.

O Israel, hope in the Lord!
For with the Lord there is mercy,
and with him is plenteous redemption.
And he will redeem Israel from all his iniquities.
Amen.

—**Psalm 130**

SESSION 1 | WHERE ARE YOU?

INTRODUCTION

Have you ever received a "wake-up call" that inspired you to make a change in your life? Maybe it was something significant like a health issue that forced you to make better choices. Or perhaps a comment from a friend convinced you to take a different course of action on something. When we go off course in life, God often sends us a wake-up call to draw us back. But sometimes it's difficult—even painful—to stop, listen, and turn around. Thankfully, God doesn't ask us to do it on our own. He not only calls us home, but he also walks with us every step of the way.

STEP 2: CONNECT

Can you share an experience that was a "wake-up" call in your life?

What do you think is the most important thing about being a Christian?

> "In the life of the body a man is sometimes sick, and unless he takes medicine, he will die. Even so in the spiritual life a man is sick on account of sin. For that reason he needs medicine so that he may be restored to health; and this grace is bestowed in the Sacrament of Penance."
>
> —St. Thomas Aquinas

Vintage alarm clock © doomu / shutterstock.com
Priest in confession booth © Anneka / shutterstock.com

STEP 3: VIDEO

Introduce and show the video episode for this session, which will last about 33 minutes. Participants can follow along with the outline in their Study Guides and take notes as key points are made during the teaching. Then discuss the questions in Step 4.

I. Wake-up Call

    A. Guilt can be God's way of getting our attention

    B. Signals that something needs to change

    C. How do we handle guilt?

        1. Find distractions

        2. Rationalize our behavior

        3. Blame others

        4. Admit we're wrong

II. Sin

    A. About breaking a relationship, not just breaking a rule

    B. Leads us to hide from God, like Adam and Eve

III. God's Perspective

    A. Above all else, God is love

    B. "Father" is who God *is*; "Lawmaker," "Judge," etc., is what he *does*

    C. "Where are you?"

        1. When we sin, God seeks us out

        2. The only sin God can't forgive is the one for which we won't ask forgiveness

"Confession is an act of honesty and courage— an act of entrusting ourselves, beyond sin, to the mercy of a loving and forgiving God. It is an act of the prodigal son who returns to his Father and is welcomed by Him with the kiss of peace."
—**Pope St. John Paul II (from a homily in San Antonio on September 13, 1987)**

SESSION 1 | WHERE ARE YOU?

STEP 4: DISCUSS

Read the following questions, giving the small groups time to answer each one. Refer to the suggested answers in italics below each question as needed to help facilitate conversation. Answers will, of course, vary.

1. What is your interpretation of this statement? "When we sin, God does not love us less, but we love ourselves less."

*(In Genesis 3:8 we read: "And they heard the sound of the L*ORD *God walking in the garden in the cool of the day, and the man and his wife hid themselves from the presence of the L*ORD *God among the trees of the garden." Adam and Eve knew of God's unconditional love for them and yet they were afraid and hid from him. What changed?* **"Man, tempted by the devil, let his trust in his Creator die in his heart"** *[CCC 397]. As a result of their sin and shame, Adam and Eve had difficulty trusting in God's love for them.)*

While God's love is unconditional, Aquinas teaches that God loves more the better thing, for the better a thing is, the more similar it is to God. Thus, while God does not love us less because of our sin, he loves us more if we do not sin, or if we are repentant of our sins.

Chain breaking © Sashkin / shutterstock.com

2. "There comes a time when one must take a position that is neither safe, nor politic, nor popular, but he must take it because conscience tells him it is right."—*Martin Luther King Jr.*, A Testament of Hope: The Essential Writings and Speeches.

In light of this quote, why is a well-formed conscience essential for our happiness?
(Sin wounds us, and virtue rewards us. Virtue is the habit of choosing the true good, which is based on a conscience formed according to the truth of the moral law, and this virtue perfects our natural freedom and increases our freedom to love. A well-formed conscience helps us to know what is true, good, and beautiful so that we can make the right choices with our actions.)

3. **"God doesn't just want more from us, he wants more for us!" What do you think this quote means?**

(It's easy to do good things because we think God wants us to check items off a to-do list: go to Mass, pray every day, stop complaining so much, go to Confession . . . and the list could go on and on. But in reality, God only asks us to do things that will increase our capacity to share in his life and love! The Catechism teaches that man is "the only creature on earth that God has willed for its own sake,' and he alone is called to share, by knowledge and love, in God's own life. It was for this end that he was created . . . " [CCC 356]. In cooperating with God's grace, we grow in our ability to resist temptation and grow in the ability to love like God does. This is the reason that we were created and the "more" God desires for us.)

> "Conscience is a judgment of reason whereby the human person recognizes the moral quality of a concrete act that he is going to perform, is in the process of performing, or has already completed."
> —CCC 1778

Man praying in church © Dzmitry Malyeuski / shutterstock.com

SESSION 1 | WHERE ARE YOU?

STEP 5: COMMIT—ENCOUNTERING GOD'S MERCY

Direct participants to the **COMMIT** *section on page 10 of their Study Guides and encourage them to spend time with this take-home assignment and be prepared to share the next time the group meets.*

Consider God's call to Adam and Eve after they had sinned: *"And they heard the sound of the L*ORD *God walking in the garden in the cool of the day, and the man and his wife hid themselves from the presence of the L*ORD *God among the trees of the garden. But the L*ORD *God called to the man, and said to him, 'Where are you?'"* (Genesis 3:8–9).

Adam and Eve's first impulse after their sin is to hide themselves from God. They feel that same guilt we experience when we know we've done something wrong, and it causes us to be separated from him. **Do you ever feel a desire to hide yourself from God? Why or why not?**

Have the participants write their reflections in the space provided in the Study Guide. When God comes to the Garden, he already knows Adam and Eve's sin. God is calling them back—out of shame and hiding, back to himself. He wants to repair the damage that sin has done. His calling out to Adam and Eve is a call to reconciliation. He wanted them to repent, accept the consequences for their wounded relationship, and, thus, be reconciled to him. While God, in his endless mercy, sought out Adam and Eve, divine justice required punishment for their sin, which includes the consequences of Original Sin both for Adam and Eve and their descendants.

God loves us so much that he won't let anything at all stand between us and his love. Before Adam and Eve have even expressed sorrow for their sin, God seeks them out. This is the incredible beauty of God's mercy! As St. Paul says in his letter to the Romans: *"But God shows his love for us in that while we were yet sinners Christ died for us"* (Romans 5:8).

God doesn't wait for us to come back to him after we have sinned—he comes looking for us, just as he looked for Adam and Eve. In his merciful love he searches for us to bring us home. He is calling to each one of us: "Where are you?" **What is your answer? What are some areas of your life that you need to surrender to God's merciful love?**

Have the participants write their reflections in the space provided in the Study Guide.

Apple © Mega Pixel / shutterstock.com

STEP 6: WRAP-UP AND CLOSING PRAYER

Here are the key points participants should take away from this session:

1. Guilt isn't a bad thing—something we should ignore or justify—but rather a wake-up call and a step toward reconciliation with God.
2. The many ways we deal with guilt, including distraction and changing our thought process to justify it, can keep us from acknowledging our sins and recognizing our need for God's forgiveness.
3. And above all else, God is a loving and merciful Father who seeks us out when we have sinned to call us back into relationship with him.

CLOSING PRAYER

Have mercy on me, O God, according to your merciful love;
according to your abundant mercy blot out my transgressions.
Wash me thoroughly from my iniquity, and cleanse me from my sin!

For I know my transgressions, and my sin is ever before me.
Against you, you only, have I sinned, and done that which is evil in your sight,
so that you are justified in your sentence and blameless in your judgment . . .

Purge me with hyssop, and I shall be clean; wash me, and I shall be whiter than snow.
Make me hear joy and gladness; let the bones which you have broken rejoice.
Hide your face from my sins, and blot out all my iniquities.

Create in me a clean heart, O God, and put a new and right spirit within me.
Cast me not away from your presence, and take not your holy Spirit from me.
Restore to me the joy of your salvation, and uphold me with a willing spirit . . .

O Lord, open my lips, and my mouth shall show forth your praise.

Amen.

—Psalm 51:1–4, 7–12, 15

FOR FURTHER STUDY

Catechism of the Catholic Church, 1422–1429

Pope St. John Paul II, *Reconciliatio et Paenitentia (Reconciliation and Penance),* Post-Synodal Apostolic Exhortation (1984)

Parable of the Prodigal Son, Luke 15:11–32

NOTES

FORGIVEN
THE TRANSFORMING POWER OF CONFESSION

SESSION 2
An Encounter with Mercy

SESSION 2 | AN ENCOUNTER WITH MERCY

> **SESSION OVERVIEW**

Read this overview in advance to familiarize yourself with the session.

In the last session we looked at how God uses our feelings of guilt as a "wake-up call" to draw us back to him in the Sacrament of Reconciliation. When sin leads us to hide from God, he comes searching for us. In this session we will look more closely at God's merciful love and how he wants to heal us in this sacrament.

The heavy burden of guilt often leads us to feel that our mistakes define us—that we are not merely sinners but that we are our sins. But this is not how God sees us. Pope St. John Paul II said, *"We are not the sum of our weaknesses and failures; we are the sum of the Father's love for us and our real capacity to become the image of his Son"* (Homily at World Youth Day in Toronto, July 28, 2002). God knows our sins, and he loves us anyway. And because of his great love for us, he continually invites us to repent and turn again to him.

Sin always damages our relationships with God and with others, and, depending on the gravity of the sin, it may rupture these relationships. This is why we need God's healing grace: because it heals those broken or damaged relationships. He calls us to the Sacrament of Reconciliation not only to forgive us and wash away our sins, but also to heal our wounds and the root causes of our sins. He does this by his own power and authority, but he wills us to do so through the mediation of the priest, another human being—so that we can encounter God's love and mercy in a very real, tangible way.

God loves us so much that he sent his Son, Jesus Christ, to die for our sins so that we might be saved. Through Baptism we are given the incredible gift of sanctifying grace, which is the divine life of God in our souls. However, this gift of sanctifying grace can be lost through mortal sin. If a sinner were to die without sanctifying grace, the consequences would be eternal separation from God (Hell). For this reason, Jesus gave us the gift of the Sacrament of Reconciliation to forgive those sins committed after Baptism.

It is important to remember that Confession is not just a place to get our slates wiped clean. It is a powerful encounter with Jesus Christ in which he pours his healing love into our hearts. It is an encounter with Mercy himself.

DIGGING DEEPER

CCC 1428 speaks about Confession as a "second conversion" for the baptized, which aims at an interior conversion of heart. This interior conversion reorients our hearts to God. It is a desire to change as we hope in God's mercy and, above all, is the work of grace. Because we still battle concupiscence (our tendency to sin), even after Baptism, the Sacrament of Reconciliation helps us to get back on track. Although it is not strictly necessary to confess less serious or venial sins, which weaken but do not destroy the life of grace in the soul, the Church strongly encourages us to confess these faults because the frequent reception of the sacrament helps to form our consciences, fight sin, and grow spiritually.

Confession is also an anticipation of the final judgment. We choose either life or death in this life, and God in his mercy wants us to be free to choose life (see CCC 1470).

SESSION OBJECTIVES

- Recognize that God is love, and his mercy comes from his tremendous love for us.
- Mercy is "the loving kindness, compassion, or forbearance shown to one who offends" (CCC, glossary).
- Understand that we encounter Christ himself in the Sacrament of Reconciliation.
- Trust that God wants to heal the root causes of our sin in Confession.
- Be strengthened by knowing that the sacrament gives us powerful grace to battle temptation and sin.

Moses and the commandments by Gustave Dore © ruskpp / shutterstock.com

SESSION 2 | AN ENCOUNTER WITH MERCY

STEP 1: OPENING PRAYER

*Begin this session by leading the **OPENING PRAYER**, which is also found in the Study Guide on page 14. Then read or summarize the **INTRODUCTION** for your group.*

Lord Jesus Christ,
You show us the glory of the Father,
the God of mercy and forgiveness,
the God who is love.
Help us to trust fully in your divine mercy
and rely completely on your unending love.
Teach us to be merciful,
as the Father is merciful,
that the whole world may know
and trust in your merciful love.
We ask this through the intercession of
Mary, Mother of Mercy.

Amen.

INTRODUCTION

God loves us right where we are, but he loves us too much to leave us there. In the last session we looked at guilt as a wake-up call—a way to turn our attention back to God when we have sinned. In this session we will look more closely at God's invitation to encounter his mercy and healing in a very real and tangible way in the Sacrament of Reconciliation.

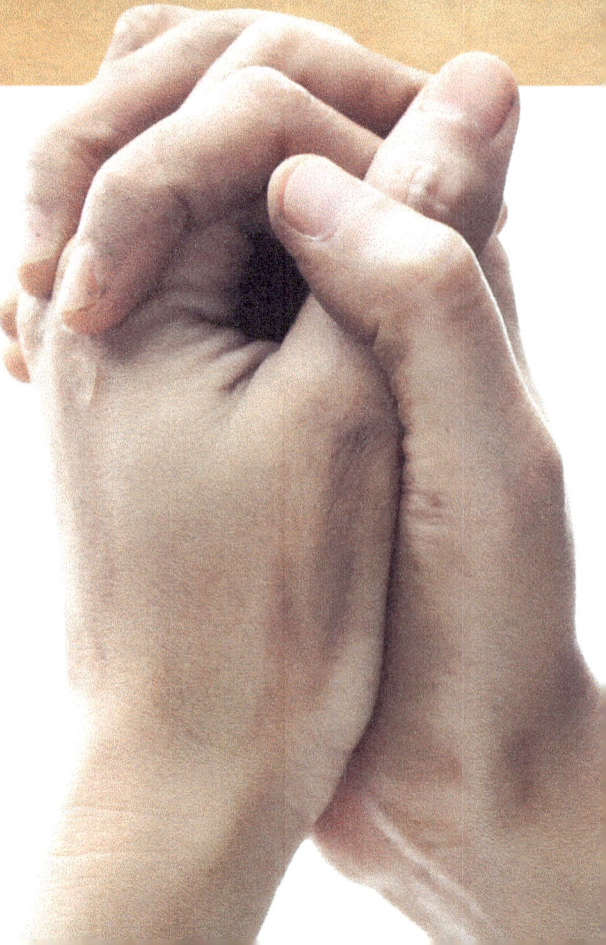

Praying hands © TairA / shutterstock.com

"Therefore, if any one is in Christ, he is a new creation; the old has passed away, behold, the new has come. All this is from God, who through Christ reconciled us to himself and gave us the ministry of reconciliation; that is, in Christ God was reconciling the world to himself, not counting their trespasses against them, and entrusting to us the message of reconciliation. So we are ambassadors for Christ, God making his appeal through us. We beg you on behalf of Christ, be reconciled to God. For our sake he made him to be sin who knew no sin, so that in him we might become the righteousness of God."

—2 Corinthians 5:17–21

STEP 2: CONNECT

Can you describe a time when you were very aware of the presence of God with you?

Who is someone that has helped you most in life?

"In her motherly care, the Church grants us the mercy of God which prevails over all our sins and is especially at work in the sacrament of reconciliation."
—CCC 2040

Lgreja de Sao Francisco de Assis © Curioso / shutterstock.com

SESSION 2 | AN ENCOUNTER WITH MERCY

> **STEP 3: VIDEO**

Introduce and show the video episode for this session, which will last about 26 minutes. Participants can follow along with the outline in their Study Guides and take notes as key points are made during the teaching. Then discuss the questions in Step 4.

I. Woman Caught in Adultery (John 8)

    A. What was she feeling?

    B. Unexpected encounter with God's love and mercy

        1. Jesus did not condemn her

        2. He also did not condone her sins

    C. God sees us as we are and loves us

    D. Confession offers a new beginning

        1. We are not our sins

        2. Mercy invites us to a much greater life

II. God's Mercy

    A. God is merciful

    B. God is constantly seeking us out

    C. We encounter Jesus himself in the Sacrament of Reconciliation

    D. Jesus gave the Apostles his own authority and power to forgive sins

        1. God has always used mediators

        2. Priest acts *in persona Christi capitis*, "in the Person of Christ the Head"

III. Human Aspect of the Sacrament

A. God knows we need a tangible experience of mercy and forgiveness

B. Confession gives us a physical encounter along with the supernatural reality of grace

C. We have a human need to say that we're sorry

D. We have a human need to actually hear someone say that we are forgiven

IV. Healing

A. In Confession Jesus forgives our sins

B. He also wants to address the root causes of our sin and heal the wounds of sin in our soul

C. The Sacrament gives us the grace to "go and sin no more"

D. God offers us his mercy so that we can extend his mercy to the world

SESSION 2 | AN ENCOUNTER WITH MERCY

STEP 4: DISCUSS

Read the following questions, giving the small groups time to answer each one. Refer to the suggested answers in italics below each question as needed to help facilitate conversation. Answers will, of course, vary.

1. According to psychologists, an identity crisis occurs when someone is unsure of their role in life and feel as if they don't really know themselves. In other words, someone experiencing an "identity crisis" is unable to provide an answer to the question "Who are you?" What difference do you think Jesus makes to the formation of a strong identity?

(Jesus proves to us that we are not defined by our failures and mistakes; rather, we are defined by God's love for us. And conversely, we are not defined by what we see as our successes either—as good as they may be, they can't make God love us more that he already does. Our identity is defined by our Baptism—in Jesus we are reconciled to God as sons and daughters of our heavenly Father.)

2. Holiness and sin have an inverse relationship. As one increases, the other decreases. That being said, it was common for many of the saints to go to Confession frequently. For example, Pope St. John Paul II and St. Teresa of Calcutta are known to have gone to Confession once a week. How do we explain this apparent contradiction?

("Sin is an offense against reason, truth, and right conscience; it is failure in genuine love for God and neighbor caused by a perverse attachment to certain goods. It wounds the nature of man and injures human solidarity. It has been defined as 'an utterance, a deed, or a desire contrary to the eternal law'" (St. Augustine, Contra Faustum 22: PL 42, 418; St. Thomas Aquinas, STh I-II, 71, 6). The effect of sin is a wound, not simply a stain on our soul. We go to the dry cleaner to clean stains but to the doctor to heal wounds. Jesus is our Divine Physician. In the sacrament, Jesus heals us of the wounds caused by sin and of the root causes of our sins. Jesus is not just wiping out our mistakes—he is giving us the grace to transform our lives. The saints, in their experience of this transformation, became more keenly aware of their wounds and desired healing.)

3. In Confession, why does the priest say "I absolve you of your sin" and not "God absolves you of your sin"?

(Jesus promised that he would remain with us: "And lo, I am with you always, to the close of the age" [Matthew 28:20]. He has fulfilled this promise through the mediation of his priests. The priest speaks for Jesus in the Sacrament of Reconciliation. St. John Vianney writes: "What is a priest? A man who holds the place of God—a man who is invested with all the powers of God." Some may object to this mediation and say "God doesn't need a priest to forgive me of my sins." That is true! But what do we need? As human beings, we have a need to experience reality through our senses. Through the mediation of the priest in the sacrament, the reality that God exists and forgives us of our sin when we repent is experienced through our senses so that we can know, deep down, that we have been reconciled to God and his Church.)

STEP 5: COMMIT—*ENCOUNTERING GOD'S MERCY*

Direct participants to the **COMMIT** *section on page 19 of their Study Guide and encourage them to spend time with this take-home assignment and be prepared to share the next time the group meets.*

The story of the woman caught in adultery in John 8:2–11 presents us with a beautiful image of the mercy and grace offered to us in the Sacrament of Reconciliation. Read through this passage slowly and prayerfully:

"Early in the morning [Jesus] came again to the temple; all the people came to him, and he sat down and taught them. The scribes and the Pharisees brought a woman who had been caught in adultery, and placing her in the midst they said to him, 'Teacher, this woman has been caught in the act of adultery. Now in the law Moses commanded us to stone such. What do you say about her?' This they said to test him, that they might have some charge to bring against him. Jesus bent down and wrote with his finger on the ground. And as they continued to ask him, he stood up and said to them, 'Let him who is without sin among you be the first to throw a stone at her.' And once more he bent down and wrote with his finger on the ground. But when they heard it, they went away, one by one, beginning with the eldest, and Jesus was left alone with the woman standing before him. Jesus looked up and said to her, 'Woman, where are they? Has no one condemned you?' She said, 'No one, Lord.' And Jesus said, 'Neither do I condemn you; go, and do not sin again.'"

—John 8:2–11

Imagine yourself in this passage. **Have you ever felt like this woman: caught in your sins, accused by others, condemning yourself for mistakes you've made? What might she have been thinking and feeling when the scribes and Pharisees brought her before Jesus to make their point? How do you think she felt when everyone else left and she was left alone with Jesus? What may have gone through her mind when she heard his words, "Neither do I condemn you; go, and do not sin again"?**

Have the participants write their reflections in the space provided in the Study Guide.

SESSION 2 | AN ENCOUNTER WITH MERCY

COMMIT - CONTINUED

Jesus rescues this woman in two ways. He forgives rather than condemns her, but he also silences her accusers. The forgiveness we receive in Confession reconciles us with God, but it also means there is no longer anything for the accuser, Satan, to hold over us. And it also means that we no longer need to accuse ourselves for our sins. They are washed away, and we are free. In place of our guilt God gives us his healing grace. Mercy makes us free to love.

God offers us his mercy so that we, in turn, can offer his mercy to a world desperately in need. **Take a few moments to prayerfully reflect on the ways God has shown you his mercy. Ask the Holy Spirit to show you one person to whom you can extend God's mercy.** This may be someone who has wronged you, someone who needs to hear the message of God's mercy, someone in need of a kind, encouraging word, etc. **What concrete thing can you do to share God's mercy with this person?**

Have the participants write their reflections in the space provided in the Study Guide.

> "My Heart overflows with great mercy for souls, and especially for poor sinners. If only they could understand that I am the best of Fathers to them and that it is for them that the Blood and Water flowed from My Heart as from a fount overflowing with mercy. For them I dwell in the tabernacle as King of Mercy."
> —Diary of St. Faustina, 367

STEP 6: WRAP-UP AND CLOSING PRAYER

Review the key points of this session together, and then end in prayer.

Here are the key points participants should take away from this session:

1. Confession is more than just a place to get absolution for our sins—it is an encounter with God's mercy.
2. In this sacrament God not only forgives us, but he also heals our wounds and the root causes of our sins.
3. It is Christ himself whom we encounter in the Sacrament of Reconciliation—the priest is acting in the Person of Christ the Head and forgiveness comes from the power and authority of Jesus.

CLOSING PRAYER

Bless the LORD, O my soul; and all that is within me, bless his holy name!
Bless the LORD, O my soul, and forget not all his benefits,
who forgives all your iniquity, who heals all your diseases,
who redeems your life from the Pit,
who crowns you with mercy and compassion,
who satisfies you with good as long as you live
so that your youth is renewed like the eagle's.

The LORD is merciful and gracious,
slow to anger and abounding in mercy.

For as high as the heavens are high above the earth,
so great is his mercy toward those who fear him;
as far as the east is from the west,
so far does he remove our transgressions from us.

Bless the LORD, O my soul!

    Amen.

—Psalm 103:1–5, 8, 11–12, 22

FOR FURTHER STUDY

Catechism of the Catholic Church, 1440-1445

John 8:1–11

Michael E. Gaitley MIC, *The Second Greatest Story Ever Told: Now Is the Time of Mercy* (Stockbridge, MA: Marian Press, 2015)

Pope Francis, *The Name of God Is Mercy* (New York: Random House, 2016)

Pope St. John Paul II, *Dives in Misericordia* (1980)

St. Maria Faustina Kowalska, *Diary: Divine Mercy in My Soul* (Stockbridge, MA: Marian Press: 2005)

Lighthouse Talks:
    Scott Hahn, *The Healing Power of Confession*
    Father Larry Richards, *Confession*

SESSION 2 | AN ENCOUNTER WITH MERCY

DIGGING DEEPER

Reflections on Divine Mercy and Justice

Can we really appreciate God's mercy and love before we recognize how we have hurt, not just ourselves, but God by our sins? Our Lady of Fatima spoke of sin as an offense against God's justice and World War II as a punishment for sins. Likewise, Saint Faustina wrote of divine justice and punishment within her beautiful exposition of God's mercy. The appeal to mercy through the Passion of Christ is not opposed to justice, but the remedy provided by God.

A sign of this is in the Parable of the Prodigal Son. His journey home includes a recognition of how he has offended his father. He begs his father for the least thing that he knows he does not deserve, and is consequently amazed to receive the gift of mercy beyond anything that he ever expected.

The Bible tells us that "the wages of sin is death, but the free gift of God is eternal life in Christ Jesus our Lord" (Rom 6:23). While we receive the gift of sanctifying grace in Baptism, this gift can be lost through mortal sin. The eternal punishment for mortal sin is eternal separation from God (Hell). This punishment is not a vengeance from an angry God but simply follows as a consequence of our sin. In his great mercy, however, God forgives this eternal punishment in the Sacrament of Reconciliation.

Divine Justice also means that there is a temporal punishment for our sins. Temporal punishment is "an unhealthy attraction to creatures, which must be purified either here on earth, or after death in the state called Purgatory" (CCC 1472). Temporal punishment should be seen as a grace, which allows us, through works of mercy and charity, and through prayer, to conform ourselves more closely to Jesus Christ.

What is an indulgence?

"An indulgence is a remission before God of the temporal punishment due to sins whose guilt has already been forgiven, which the faithful Christian who is duly disposed gains under certain prescribed conditions through the action of the Church which, as the minister of redemption, dispenses and applies with authority the treasury of the satisfactions of Christ and the saints" (Paul VI, apostolic constitution, *Indulgentiarum doctrina*, Norm 1).

"An indulgence is partial or plenary according as it removes either part or all of the temporal punishment due to sin" (*Indulgentiarum doctrina*, Norm 2; cf. Norm 3). The faithful can gain indulgences for themselves or apply them to the dead (see CIC, can. 994).

FORGIVEN™
THE TRANSFORMING POWER OF CONFESSION

SESSION 3
The Rite Explained

SESSION 3 | THE RITE EXPLAINED

SESSION OVERVIEW

Read this overview in advance to familiarize yourself with the session.

The God who created us knows exactly what we need—and he offers it to us in the Sacrament of Reconciliation. In the last session we looked at the depth and beauty of God's mercy. We saw that we are not defined by our mistakes; we are defined by the Father's love for us. And in his great love, God desires to truly heal us as well as cleanse us of our sins in Confession. In this session we will look more closely at the Rite of Penance and how we can prepare ourselves to receive it.

God, in his wisdom and mercy, has given us a beautiful gift in the Sacrament of Reconciliation. In the Rite of Penance, we find both a human experience of sorrow and forgiveness as well as a real divine encounter and the spiritual reality of grace and healing. While the human aspect of it often makes us feel uncomfortable—no one likes to list all of their failures and mistakes for someone else to hear—the priests who share their perspective on the sacrament assure us that it is a joy and a privilege to witness this intimate encounter of forgiveness and healing.

In the Rite of Penance, Christ's paschal mystery is made mystically present to us through a liturgical act. It is God's act of blessing, giving us real graces that heal us and allow us to grow in the Christian life. It's not just a human experience of forgiveness. The sacramental reality goes much deeper than this because it applies the fruits of Christ's Passion and Resurrection directly to our own lives. Each step of the Rite speaks to the reality of God's presence in the sacrament and the power of his mercy. This is why preparation for the sacrament is so important. In order to be fully open to the grace God offers us, we must carefully examine our lives and approach him with both humility and trust.

DIGGING DEEPER

Some wounds are deeper than others. Because mortal sin destroys the life of grace in the soul and ruptures our relationship to God and his Church, we need God's minister (the priest) to absolve us formally when we've committed mortal sin. Confession is the ordinary means of forgiveness in the Church and one of the precepts of the Church requires us to confess mortal sins at least once a year. Mortal sins must also be confessed according to number and kind (see *CIC*, 988).

> Anyone who is aware of having committed a mortal sin should not receive the Eucharist, even if he thinks he has perfect contrition, without first receiving absolution in the Sacrament of Reconciliation.
> (see CCC 1856–1859, 1452–1453, 1457)

SESSION OBJECTIVES

- Understand why we shouldn't be afraid or embarrassed to go to Confession.
- Recognize that sins can be mortal or venial, committed in thought, word, action, and inaction.
- Learn how to prepare for the Sacrament of Reconciliation by making an examination of conscience.
- Understand the order and different steps of the Rite of Penance and what they mean and accomplish.

Confessional © Ivan U / shutterstock.com

SESSION 3 | THE RITE EXPLAINED

STEP 1: OPENING PRAYER

*Begin this session by leading the **OPENING PRAYER**, which is also found in the Study Guide on page 24. Then read or summarize the **INTRODUCTION** for your group.*

Blessed is he whose transgression
is forgiven, whose sin is covered.
Blessed is the man to whom the LORD
imputes no iniquity,
and in whose spirit there is no deceit.
When I declared not my sin,
my body wasted away through my groaning all day long.
For day and night your hand was heavy upon me;
my strength was dried up as by the heat of summer.
I acknowledged my sin to you, and I did not hide my iniquity;
I said, "I will confess my transgressions to the LORD";
then you forgave the guilt of my sin.
Therefore let every one who is godly offer prayer to you;
at a time of distress, in the rush of great waters,
they shall not reach him.
You are a hiding place for me,
you preserve me from trouble;
you surround me with deliverance.

—Psalm 32:1–7

INTRODUCTION

It's not easy to admit when we've done something wrong—or failed to do something right. But when we learn to trust in God's mercy, we don't have to be afraid to face our sins. That mercy is present to us in a very real way in the confessional through the ministry of the priest. God's merciful love shapes every word and action of the sacrament, and when we prepare for it honestly and prayerfully, we will be open to receiving the fullness of his grace.

STEP 2: CONNECT

Can you describe a time when you had to take a risk and trust?

What would you like the courage to do?

"He who conceals his transgressions will not prosper, but he who confesses and forsakes them will obtain mercy."
—**Proverbs 28:13**

Confession booth © Viktor1 / shutterstock.com

SESSION 3 | THE RITE EXPLAINED

STEP 3: VIDEO

Introduce and show the video episode for this session, which will last about 33 minutes. Participants can follow along with the outline in their Study Guides and take notes as key points are made during the teaching.

I. Priests' Perspective on Confession

    A. It's a joy and privilege to welcome people back to God in the sacrament

    B. Nothing new under the sun—you aren't going to shock the priest with your sin

    C. Absolutely confidential (Seal of Confession)

    D. Admiration for the courage of the penitent

    E. Many priests forget everything they hear in the confessional

    F. Sin is forgiven to make us free to love

II. The Sacrament

    A. Examination of Conscience

        1. We prepare for the sacrament because we take the encounter with Christ seriously

        2. Consider what sins we have committed

        3. Keep in mind that we are approaching our loving Father

        4. "In my thoughts"—our words and actions have their root in our thoughts

        5. "In my words"—we can sin through our speech

        6. "In what I have done"—sins of commission; what we most commonly consider as sin

        7. "In what I have failed to do"—sins of omission

    B. Sign of the Cross

    C. "Bless me Father, for I have sinned. It has been … since my last confession"—gives the priest context

    D. State our sins

        1. Simple, straightforward, honest

        2. Humbling but not humiliating

        3. List first your mortal sins according to number and kind, and if you forget a venial sin don't worry because it can be forgiven in other ways, such as through an act of contrition.

E. Penance

    1. Act of love and thanksgiving in response to God's forgiveness

    2. Addresses some of the practical consequences of sin

F. Act of Contrition

    1. Like a formal apology

    2. Can use a memorized prayer or make up your own

G. Absolution

    1. Priest raises both hands (or at least his right hand) over penitent—invokes God's presence

    2. Recites the prayer of Absolution—this is the moment of forgiveness

        a. Father of mercies

        b. Pardon and peace

        c. Ministry of the Church

Whenever we make an examination of conscience, we can also look at other aspects of sin to see what we should bring to Confession. The *Catechism* tells us that we can distinguish between sins: (1) according to their object, the virtues they oppose, or the commandments they violate; (2) whether they concern God, neighbor, or self; (3) whether they are spiritual or carnal sins; and (4) whether they relate to thought, word, deed, or omission **(see CCC 1853).**

Mortal and Venial Sins

Mortal sin . . . results in the loss of charity and the privation of sanctifying grace, that is, of the state of grace. If it is not redeemed by repentance and God's forgiveness, it causes exclusion from Christ's kingdom and the eternal death of hell. (CCC 1861)

For a sin to be mortal, three conditions must together be met: "Mortal sin is sin whose object is grave matter and which is also committed with full knowledge and deliberate consent" (*RP* 17 § 12). (CCC 1857)

One commits venial sin when, in a less serious matter, he does not observe the standard prescribed by the moral law, or when he disobeys the moral law in a grave matter, but without full knowledge or without complete consent. (CCC 1862)

Venial sin weakens charity; it manifests a disordered affection for created goods; it impedes the soul's progress in the exercise of the virtues and the practice of the moral good; it merits temporal punishment. (CCC 1863)

SESSION 3 | THE RITE EXPLAINED

STEP 4: DISCUSS

Read the following questions, giving the small groups time to answer each one. Refer to the suggested answers in italics below each question as needed to help facilitate conversation. Answers will, of course, vary.

1. In the video we heard that God forgives our sin in order to clear the way for love. Grace increases in our souls similar to the way a fire increases in brightness and heat with the addition of more fuel. Since sanctifying grace is God's very life, how are we to understand an increase of God's life within us when he is already omnipresent and infinite?

*("It is not possible to get more of God. Rather, our soul's capacity to absorb his life and love increases. This is where we exercise our freedom. We can choose to grow in grace or not. In James 4:6 we read: **"But he gives more grace"** and **"God opposes the proud, but gives grace to the humble."** The humble recognize their sin and their need for God's forgiveness and grace. The humble are able to say what can be the most difficult words to say in our relationship with God and with others: "I'm sorry! Will you forgive me?" Frequent Confession helps us to grow in humility and charity.)*

2. God's will for our lives is to grow in self-awareness, self-possession, and self-donation. In other words, it is difficult to give ourselves away in love if we are not free to love. And, it is difficult to grow in the freedom necessary to love if we are not aware of what restrains us. How does understanding the purpose of our lives emphasize the importance of a good examination of conscience?

*("The world promises you comfort, but you were not made for comfort. You were made for greatness" [Pope Benedict XVI]. We have a high calling as Christians. A well-formed conscience helps us to understand who we are called to be. A good examination of conscience is taking the time to reflect on the ways we are failing to live up to that calling through our thoughts, words, actions, or omissions. The more we are aware of our failings and the source of those failings, the more empowered we are to overcome them. And, this makes us more grateful for the Sacrament of Reconciliation where we experience what St. Paul writes to the Philippians: **"In our weakness, he is strong"** [2 Corinthians 12:10].)*

Confession by Roehn © Restored Traditions. All rights reserved.

3. A presidential candidate was asked the question: "How do you define sin?" His answer was: "Being out of alignment with my values." What is problematic with this answer?

*(This answer is an example of relativism. Relativism is a worldview that denies the existence of objective truth. In other words, there are no universal "rights or wrongs" that we can know, live by, and promote. Therefore, truth is what an individual decides it to be. In this system of thought, we are free to do as we please as long it does not "hurt others." The Catechism, quoting St. Augustine, teaches that sin is **"an utterance, a deed, or a desire contrary to the eternal law"** [1849]. God has given us his eternal law out of his great love for us. When you love people, you tell them the truth. The prevalence of relativism has created a great obstacle to grace: the loss of the sense of sin. Pope Pius XII said in the wake of the horrors of World War II that "the greatest sin today is that men have lost the sense of sin.")*

> "Confession heals, confession justifies, confession grants pardon of sin, all hope consists in confession; in confession there is a chance for mercy."
>
> —**St. Isidore of Seville**

SESSION 3 | THE RITE EXPLAINED

STEP 5: COMMIT—*ENCOUNTERING GOD'S MERCY*

Direct participants to the COMMIT section on page 29 of their Study Guides, and encourage them to spend time with this take-home assignment and be prepared to share the next time the group meets.

An examination of conscience is a prayerful reflection on our life, looking for sins that we might have committed in our thoughts, words, actions, or inaction. There are many different kinds of examinations of conscience—some are structured around the Ten Commandments; some are based on the seven capital (or deadly) sins. A simple way to begin looking for sin is to look at our thoughts, words, actions, and inaction through the lens of the two greatest commandments: **"The first is, 'Hear, O Israel: The Lord our God, the Lord is one; and you shall love the Lord your God with all your heart, and with all your soul, and with all your mind, and with all your strength.' The second is this, 'You shall love your neighbor as yourself'"** (Mark 12:29–31). Take some time in quiet prayer to reflect on these verses. Begin by asking the Holy Spirit to help you make this examination of conscience:

Spirit of truth, guide me as I examine my life. Give me the wisdom to see all my thoughts, words, actions, and inaction as you do. Give me the courage to acknowledge my sins. Give me the humility and strength to confess my sins. And give me the grace to trust wholeheartedly in your mercy and forgiveness. Amen.

Prayerfully consider, **"In what ways have I not loved God with my whole heart, soul, mind, and strength? In what ways have I failed to love my neighbor as myself?"**

Have the participants write their reflections in the space provided in the Study Guide.

What do you think it means to see our sins the way God sees them?

Have the participants write their reflections in the space provided in the Study Guide.

> *"Go to your confessor; open your heart to him; display to him all the recesses of your soul; take the advice that he will give you with the utmost humility and simplicity. For God, who has an infinite love for obedience, frequently renders profitable the counsels we take from others, but especially from those who are the guides of our souls."*
> —St. Francis de Sales

STEP 6: WRAP-UP AND CLOSING PRAYER

Review the key points of this session together, and then end in prayer.

Here are the key points participants should take away from this session:

1. Priests generally find great joy in hearing confessions because they get to witness God's powerful mercy truly changing lives.
2. You won't shock or scandalize a priest with your confession, and he won't think any less of you for the sins you have confessed.
3. Confession is completely confidential because the priest is bound by the Seal of Confession.
4. The sacrament requires thoughtful preparation, which we call an examination of conscience.
5. Mortal sin is serious sin that completely ruptures our relationship to God and requires us to go to Confession before receiving the Eucharist. There are three things necessary for a sin to be mortal: (1) grave matter, (2) full knowledge, and (3) full consent.
6. The Rite of Penance includes the Sign of the Cross, listing your sins, receiving your penance, making an Act of Contrition, and receiving absolution. Although not in the Rite of Penance, it is a good and praiseworthy custom for penitents to state how long it has been since their last Confession.
7. The three acts of the penitent are contrition, confession, and satisfaction.

    Contrition is an inner disposition of the heart, which includes purpose of amendment, before it is expressed in the Act of Contrition.

    Confession is telling your sins to the priest, and satisfaction or penance is an act of love in response to forgiveness—it is not a way to earn forgiveness.

    All three acts of the penitent must be present in a confession in order for the confessor to impart sacramental absolution.

SESSION 3 | THE RITE EXPLAINED

CLOSING PRAYER

The Confiteor

I confess to almighty God,
and to you, my brothers and sisters,
that I have greatly sinned,
in my thoughts and in my words,
in what I have done and in what I have failed to do,
through my fault, through my fault,
through my most grievous fault;
therefore I ask blessed Mary ever-Virgin,
all the Angels and Saints,
and you, my brothers and sisters,
to pray for me to the Lord our God.

Amen.

—*Roman Missal*, 4

Outdoor confessionals in Krakow, Poland, prepared for the World Youth Day 2016 © Nahlik / shutterstock.com

FOR FURTHER STUDY

Catechism of the Catholic Church, 1480–1484, 1846–1869

Christopher Walsh, *The Untapped Power of the Sacrament of Penance: A Priest's View* (Cincinnati, OH: Servant Books, 2005)

Go to USCCB.org to find several examinations of conscience in the Prayer and Worship/Sacraments section

John A. Kane, *How to Make a Good Confession: A Pocket Guide to Reconciliation with God* (Manchester, NH: Sophia Institute Press, 2001)

Augustine Institute: *How to Make a Good Confession* Booklet

Lighthouse Talks: *7 Secrets of Confession* by Vinny Flynn

Examination of Conscience Based on the Ten Commandments

1. I am the LORD your God. You shall have no false gods before me. Do I put God before my spouse? My children? My work? Do I believe that God loves me? Do I have any "false gods" in my life like money, fame, power, possessions? Have I been involved in fortune-telling, astrology, palm-reading, or witchcraft? Do I pray daily?

2. You shall not take the name of the LORD your God in vain. Do I use curse words? Have I made oaths or sworn promises to God that I haven't kept? Have I allowed others to swear in my presence?

3. Remember to keep holy the LORD's Day. Do I attend Mass on Sundays and Holy Days of Obligation? Do I avoid unnecessary work on Sundays? Do I avoid unnecessary shopping on Sundays?

4. Honor your father and mother. Do I show love to my parents, regardless of their age? Do I help them when I can? Do I respect my employer and others in authority? If I am a parent, have I given a bad example in word or deed to my children? Am I raising my children in the Catholic Faith?

5. You shall not kill. Have I killed or seriously injured anyone? Do I gossip? Have I had an abortion or helped someone get an abortion? Have I lost my temper, given in to anger, or harbored resentment against my neighbor? Do I bear grudges? Have I ever harmed anyone physically, mentally, or emotionally? Do I take care of the environment?

6. You shall not commit adultery. Have I had premarital sex, whether with someone of the same or opposite sex? Have I treated anyone as an object, rather than a person? Have I used contraception or IVF? (or have I cooperated with my spouse in doing so?) Have I been unfaithful to my spouse in my thoughts, desires, or actions? Have I used my wife or husband merely to satisfy my sexual urges? Have I masturbated? Do I eat or drink in excess? Have I lost sobriety through drunkenness or drug use?

7. You shall not steal. Have I stolen anything? Do I always give a full day's work for a full day's pay? Do I cheat in school or business? Am I fair in paying my employees? Am I honest in paying my taxes? Have I wasted time? Have I been generous in serving the poor?

8. You shall not bear false witness against your neighbor. Have I told a lie, even a white lie? Have I told lies to avoid getting in trouble? Have I revealed other people's secrets? Have I failed to mind my own business? Have I accused someone falsely? Have I judged others harshly? Have I been prejudiced or discriminated against anyone?

9. You shall not covet your neighbor's wife. Have I consented to impure thoughts or desires? Have I looked willingly at others in an impure manner? Have I view pornography or watched movies that are overly violent or sexual? Have I spoken in an unchaste way or willingly listened to impure speech? Have I been envious or jealous of others, or gossiped and been overly curious?

10. You shall not covet your neighbor's property. Have I envied anyone else's possessions, money, fame, or success? Have I used more than my fair share of resources?

Precepts of the Catholic Church

1. Attend Mass on Sundays and Holy Days of Obligation.
2. Confess your [mortal] sins at least once a year.
3. Receive the Sacrament of the Eucharist, at least during the Easter season.
4. Observe the days of fasting and abstinence established by the Church.
5. Help provide for the needs of the Church.
6. Observe the Church's laws on marriage.

NOTES

FORGIVEN
THE TRANSFORMING POWER OF CONFESSION

SESSION 4
Biblical Foundations: Sin, Mercy, and the Sacrament of Confession

SESSION 4 | BIBLICAL FOUNDATIONS: SIN, MERCY, AND THE SACRAMENT OF CONFESSION

> **SESSION OVERVIEW**

Read this overview in advance to familiarize yourself with the session.

In the last session we took a closer look at what we say and do in Confession. We have examined this sacrament from the point of view of both the priest and the penitent, but two foundational questions still remain: What is the scriptural background for the Sacrament of Reconciliation? And why did Christ choose to offer his forgiveness through the ministry of the priesthood?

For many people, the Old Testament and the New Testament seem to paint two completely different pictures of God. With all the war and punishments and curses in the Old Testament, it can be easy to assume that God is wrathful and quick to judge when his people don't live up to his exacting standards. On the other hand, the familiar stories of the New Testament make God's love and mercy very clear. A closer look at Scripture, however, quickly dispels the error that God is harsh and angry in the Old Testament and shows how God is consistently patient and merciful with his people. The reality and power of God's forgiveness is demonstrated in a particular way in the life of King David, who models for us true contrition and absolute confidence in God's mercy.

This careful reading of Scripture also demonstrates that in both the Old and New Testaments God delegates his authority, first to angels, and then to men. When we see the scriptural pattern of angels and men receiving authority from God to speak and to act for him, it becomes clear that the priest speaking and acting for Christ in the Sacrament of Reconciliation is not a human invention but rather a divine ministry.

Scripture shows us that we can have total confidence in God's merciful love and in the reality of his forgiveness. God doesn't just discount or ignore our sins—he completely wipes them away. There is no limit to his forgiveness. And our confidence comes not just from our own faith, but through the gift of hearing God himself speak through the ministry of the priesthood when we hear the words of absolution.

SESSION OBJECTIVES

- Be familiar with the attributes God reveals in Exodus 34:6–7.
- Understand that the Old Testament reveals and emphasizes God's loving mercy and forgiveness.
- Recognize the model of true contrition and confidence in God's mercy in David's life.
- Understand the pattern of God delegating his authority to angels and men in Scripture and how that sets the foundation for the authority of the priest to speak and act for God in Confession.

STEP 1: OPENING PRAYER

Begin this session by leading the **OPENING PRAYER,** *which is also found in the Study Guide on page 34. Then read or summarize the* **INTRODUCTION** *for your group.*

Hear my prayer, O LORD; give ear to my supplications!
In thy faithfulness answer me, in your righteousness!
Enter not into judgment with your servant;
for no man living is righteous before you.

For the enemy has pursued me; he has crushed my life to the ground; he has made me sit in darkness like those long dead. Therefore my spirit faints within me; my heart within me is appalled.

I remember the days of old, I meditate on all that you have done; I muse on what your hands have wrought. I stretch out my hands to you; my soul thirsts for you like a parched land.

Make haste to answer me, O LORD! My spirit fails!
Hide not your face from me, lest I be like those who go down to the Pit. Let me hear in the morning of your merciful love, for in you I put my trust. Teach me the way I should go, for to you I lift up my soul.

Amen.

—Psalm 143:1–8

SESSION 4 | BIBLICAL FOUNDATIONS: SIN, MERCY, AND THE SACRAMENT OF CONFESSION

INTRODUCTION

Have you ever wondered, "Where is *that* in the Bible?!" When it comes to the Sacrament of Reconciliation, Catholics and non-Catholics alike often want to know how confessing our sins to a priest lines up with Scripture passages such as **"Who can forgive sins but God alone?"** (Mark 2:7). Confession has its roots in God's revelation of his mercy as well as his authority in Scripture—and a closer look quickly shows just how biblical this sacrament really is.

STEP 2: CONNECT

How has your perception of God changed from your childhood to the present?

How has your perception of yourself changed from your childhood to the present?

> "Pray with great confidence, with confidence based upon the goodness and infinite generosity of God and upon the promises of Jesus Christ. God is a spring of living water which flows unceasingly into the hearts of those who pray."
>
> —St. Louis de Montfort

The Bible © Billion Photos / shutterstock.com

STEP 3: VIDEO

Introduce and show the video episode for this first part, which will last about 30 minutes. Participants can follow along with the outline in their Study Guides and take notes as key points are made during the teaching. Then discuss the questions in Step 4.

PART I

I. Sin and Mercy in Scripture

A. Adam and Eve sinned, and God showed them mercy

B. This pattern is repeated throughout Scripture: Israel sins, and God responds with mercy

C. Greatest example is at Mount Sinai

II. Exodus 34:6–7

A. Becomes one of the most important passages in the Old Testament

B. Eight key attributes of God

1. Merciful
2. Gracious
3. Slow to Anger
4. Abounding in steadfast love
5. Faithfulness
6. Storing up steadfast love for 1,000 generations
7. Forgiving iniquity and transgression and sin
8. Does not clear the guilty (those who don't ask for forgiveness)

C. All the prophetic books quote this passage to remind Israel of God's mercy

III. *Shuv*

A. "Repentance" in Hebrew

B. Literally "to turn about"

C. Repentance is about changing from our way to God's way

Manager delegates work to team © Jirsak / shutterstock.com

SESSION 4 | BIBLICAL FOUNDATIONS: SIN, MERCY, AND THE SACRAMENT OF CONFESSION

VIDEO CONTINUED

IV. David

    A. Greatly blessed and favored by God

    B. But then he commits adultery and murders to cover it up

    C. David admits his sin and repents (2 Samuel 12)—in contrast to Saul who denies his sin

    D. David has courage to confess because he has hope in God's mercy

        1. Psalm 51:1—**"Have mercy on me, O God"**

        2. Themes of mercy and forgiveness in Psalm 51 echo attributes of God revealed in Exodus 34:6–7

    E. David shows us what it means to trust in God's forgiveness

        1. David's last words, 2 Samuel 22 (also Psalm 18)

        2. 2 Samuel 22:21–27—David says he is blameless and pure

        3. He can say this because he trusts that God's forgiveness truly cleanses him from his sin

        4. Psalm 103:12—**"As far as the east is from the west, so far does he remove our transgressions from us"**

V. Exile

    A. Nehemiah 9—Ezra reminds the people of Exodus 34:6–7 and the pattern of Israel's sin and God's forgiveness

    B. Exile is the physical manifestation of the reality of sin—being far from God

    C. The return from exile is the *shuv*—the people are brought back to Jerusalem as a sign of repentance and returning to God

    D. The real scandal of Scripture is God's mercy

You may take a break after watching the first part then show the video episode for this second part, which will last about 35 minutes.

PART II

I. Why do we confess our sins to a priest?

　A. Matthew 9:1–8—the paralytic lowered through the roof of Peter's house

　　1. Physical healing is a sign that Jesus also has the power and authority to forgive sins

　　2. Son of man—reference to Daniel 7:13–14

　　3. **"They glorified God, who had given such authority to men"** (Matthew 9:8)

　B. Authority in Matthew's Gospel

　　1. Matthew 8–9 shows Jesus's authority through ten miracles

　　2. Number ten signifies authority

　　3. Jesus has authority from the Father, and he has the authority to delegate that authority

　　4. Matthew 10—Jesus gives his authority to the twelve Apostles and sends them out

　C. Authority in Luke's Gospel

　　1. Luke 10—Jesus sends out seventy disciples with his authority

　　2. Jesus sends his disciples as his ambassadors—they speak his words

　　3. 2 Corinthians 5:18–20—Paul talks about his ministry as an ambassador of Christ's reconciliation

　D. Authority in John's Gospel

　　1. John 17:18—Jesus sends the Apostles as the Father sent him *(apostello,* Greek meaning "to send")

　　2. In the Old Testament, the angels bear the presence and word of God, speaking and acting on his behalf

　　3. In the New Testament, the Apostles now bear the presence and word of God, speaking and acting on his behalf

　　4. Jesus shares his divine authority with men

　　5. John 20:22–23—Jesus gives his Apostles authority to forgive sins

SESSION 4 | BIBLICAL FOUNDATIONS: SIN, MERCY, AND THE SACRAMENT OF CONFESSION

STEP 4: DISCUSS

Read the following questions, giving the small groups time to answer each one. Refer to the suggested answers in italics below each question as needed to help facilitate conversation. Answers will, of course, vary.

1. Author Richard Dawkins writes in *The God Delusion:* "The God of the Old Testament is arguably the most unpleasant character in all fiction." As an atheist, Dawkins writes this to undermine Christianity and the Bible. How can we reconcile the God of the Old Testament and the merciful love of our heavenly Father revealed to us through Jesus Christ?

(Pope Benedict XVI writes: "God's plan is manifested progressively and it is accomplished slowly, in successive stages and despite human resistance. God chose a people and patiently worked to guide and educate them" [Verbum Domini, 42]. In other words, God progressively revealed his character to a people who lived in warlike times. Even so, his revelation of himself on Mount Sinai reveals that he is "a God merciful and gracious, slow to anger, and abounding in steadfast love and faithfulness" [Exodus 34:6]. The Catechism teaches: "Christians therefore read the Old Testament in the light of Christ crucified and risen" [129]. Therefore, we interpret the Old Testament through the lens of the life and teaching of Jesus Christ.)

2. God says this of David, the great king of Israel: *"I have found in David the son of Jesse a man after my heart, who will do all my will"* (Acts 13:22). And yet, David failed miserably in doing God's will when he committed adultery with Bathsheba and had her husband killed so that he could take her to be his wife. Given these circumstances, how is David a role model for us?

(The Book of Hebrews compares the Christian life to a race: "Let us run with perseverance the race that is set before us, looking to Jesus the pioneer and perfecter of our faith . . ." [12:1–2]. David is an example to us that our sin, no matter how grave, does not disqualify us from the race. Sin knocks us down, but God calls us to get back up and run even harder. Psalm 51 reveals the depths of David's sorrow and his total confidence in God's mercy and forgiveness. It shows how David overcomes his pride, the difficulty we have accepting our failings and forgiving ourselves, and offers to the Lord a contrite heart.)

3. The great rabbi Maimonides is credited with this profound statement: "Give a man a fish and you feed him for a day; teach a man to fish and you feed him for a lifetime." How does this statement give insight into the reasons Jesus delegated his priesthood?

(The priest is an ambassador because he speaks and acts with the authority of Christ—not his own. What he says and does in the Sacrament of Reconciliation is in the Person of Christ the Head, so if we reject him, we are rejecting Christ. Some participants will have already heard this, and so it may not change their attitude. Others may learn to look past the priest as a man and see Jesus in the sacrament. They may feel more comfortable with the idea of the priest's authority once they understand that the priest's authority to forgive sins comes not from himself or his own merit, but from God's authority and free gift. Thinking about this delegation of authority can also lead us to greater awe and wonder in contemplating God's mercy.)

> "God's patience has to call forth in us the courage to return to him, however many mistakes and sins there may be in our life. . . . It is there, in the wounds of Jesus, that we are truly secure; there we encounter the boundless love of his heart. Thomas understood this. Saint Bernard goes on to ask: But what can I count on? My own merits? No, 'My merit is God's mercy. I am by no means lacking merits as long as he is rich in mercy. If the mercies of the Lord are manifold, I too will abound in merits.' This is important: the courage to trust in Jesus' mercy, to trust in his patience, to seek refuge always in the wounds of his love."
>
> —Pope Francis, *Homily on Divine Mercy Sunday*, April 7, 2013

SESSION 4 | BIBLICAL FOUNDATIONS: SIN, MERCY, AND THE SACRAMENT OF CONFESSION

STEP 5: COMMIT—ENCOUNTERING GOD'S MERCY

*Direct participants to the **COMMIT** section on page 40 of their Study Guides, and encourage them to spend time with this take-home assignment and be prepared to share the next time the group meets.*

In the video Tim Gray said that Exodus 34:6–7 becomes the most important passage in the Old Testament for understanding who God is. Read through this passage two or three times slowly and prayerfully.

"The Lord passed before him, and proclaimed, 'The Lord, the Lord, a God merciful and gracious, slow to anger, and abounding in mercy and faithfulness, keeping merciful love for thousands, forgiving iniquity and transgression and sin, but who will by no means clear the guilty." (Exodus 34:6–7)

Which of the eight key characteristics of God revealed in this passage stands out the most to you? Why?

Have the participants write their reflections in the space provided in the Study Guide.

Psalm 18 is a prayer of David thanking God for delivering him from his physical enemy, Saul. When he prayed it again at the end of his life, David surely understood the necessity of thanking God not only for rescuing him physically throughout his life but, even more importantly, delivering him from his sins. Read through Psalm 18, and then compose your own short psalm of thanksgiving to God for his saving mercy toward you.

STEP 6: WRAP-UP AND CLOSING PRAYER

Review the key points of this session together, and then end in prayer.

Here are the key points participants should take away from this session:

1. The revelation of God's mercy and abundant love in Exodus 34:6–7 and the repetition of this theme throughout the Old Testament.

2. The model that David provides for confessing our sins and trusting in God's forgiveness.

3. The pattern of God delegating his authority to angels in the Old Testament and men in the New Testament, and specifically the authority to forgive sins delegated to the Apostles in John 20.

King David kneeling before God
© Restored Traditions. All rights reserved.

CLOSING PRAYER

Let's close our time together in prayer:

I love you, O LORD, my strength.
The LORD is my rock, and my fortress, and my deliverer,
my God, my rock, in whom I take refuge,
my shield, and the horn of my salvation, my stronghold.
I call upon the LORD, who is worthy to be praised,
and I am saved from my enemies.

The LORD rewarded me according to my righteousness;
according to the cleanness of my hands he recompensed me.
For I have kept the ways of the LORD, and have not wickedly departed from my God.
For all his ordinances were before me, and his statues I did not put away from me.
I was blameless before him, and I kept myself from guilt.
Therefore the LORD has recompensed me according to my righteousness,
according to the cleanness of my hands in his sight.

With the loyal you show yourself loyal;
with the blameless man you show yourself blameless;
with the pure you show yourself pure;
and with the crooked you show yourself perverse.
For you deliver a humble people; but the haughty eyes you bring down.
Yes, you light my lamp; the LORD my God lightens my darkness.
Yes, by you I can crush a troop; and by my God I can leap over a wall.
This God—his way is perfect; the promise of the LORD proves true;
he is a shield for all those who take refuge in him.

Amen.

—Psalm 18:1–3, 20–30

FOR FURTHER STUDY

Tim Gray, "Sacrament of Penance and Reconciliation" in *Sacraments in Scripture: Salvation History Made Present* (Steubenville, OH: Emmaus Road Publishing, 2001)

Scott Hahn, *Lord Have Mercy: The Healing Power of Confession* (New York: Doubleday, 2003)

Catechism of the Catholic Church on the Sacrament of Penance and Reconciliation, 1440–1445

NOTES

FORGIVEN™
THE TRANSFORMING POWER OF CONFESSION

SESSION 5
Answering Common Questions about Confession

SESSION 5 | ANSWERING COMMON QUESTIONS ABOUT CONFESSION

SESSION OVERVIEW

Read this overview in advance to familiarize yourself with the session.

We took a detailed look at the scriptural basis for the Sacrament of Reconciliation in the last session. In this final session we will touch on many of the ideas already mentioned in the early sessions to make sure that the answers to some of the most common questions about Confession are clear to the participants. These answers begin and end with love—the source and foundation of this sacrament.

People have many questions about the Sacrament of Reconciliation. Some of these questions have very simple and straightforward answers. "What do I do in the sacrament?" "How do I prepare for making my confession?" Other questions require lengthier answers pulling from Scripture and the teachings of the Church. "What does Confession accomplish?" "Why confess to a priest?" And some questions might not even occur to people as having anything in particular to do with Confession. "Who is God?" "What is his nature?" "How do we know him?" But the Sacrament of Reconciliation flows directly out of God's nature of steadfast love and mercy, and so any explanation of the sacrament must first start with a firm understanding of who God is and what he wants for us. In addition to understanding that "God is love," it is also important to realize that "God is truth." Jesus came to teach us the truth about God and how we are to live in the kingdom that he was to establish.

In fact, the answer to any question about Confession is much more than a Bible verse or a line from Church teaching. The answer to every single question about the sacrament is part of a story, the narrative of God's love for us and his plan to save us from our sins and bring us back into relationship with him.

SESSION OBJECTIVES

- Understand that Confession flows directly from God's inner nature of love.
- Recognize that priests have authority to act as mediators for God in virtue of the authority that Jesus granted to the Apostles that has been passed down to them.
- Learn how the peace of forgiveness helps us to thrive.
- Understand what happens during Confession.

STEP 1: OPENING PRAYER

*Begin this session by leading the **OPENING PRAYER**, which is also found in the Study Guide on page 44. Then read or summarize the **INTRODUCTION** for your group.*

Lord God,
I hope by your grace for the pardon of all my sins
And after life here to gain eternal happiness
Because you have promised it
Who are infinitely powerful, faithful, kind, and merciful.
In this hope I intend to live and die.

Amen.

—Act of Hope

INTRODUCTION

In 1 John 4:8 we read that **"God is love."** This is the beginning of the answer to every possible question about the Sacrament of Reconciliation. Over the course of this study we have looked at God's love and mercy, how he seeks us out and calls us back to himself when we sin, how to prepare for and participate in the Sacrament of Reconciliation, and where we find its basis in Scripture. It all begins in God's love for us and his desire to forgive and heal us in this sacrament. Why do we need to go to a priest? Why is the sacrament designed the way that it is? The first part of the answer is: because God is love.

SESSION 5 | ANSWERING COMMON QUESTIONS ABOUT CONFESSION

STEP 2: CONNECT

Have you identified a particular calling or purpose for your life?

What appeals to you most about spending eternity in Heaven?

> "Our Lord Himself I saw in . . . this venerable Sacrament . . . I felt as if my chains fell, as those of St. Peter at the touch of the Divine messenger. My God, what new scenes for my soul!"
> —St. Elizabeth Ann Seton

STEP 3: VIDEO

Introduce and show the video episode for this session, which will last about 38 minutes. Participants can follow along with the outline in their Study Guides and take notes as key points are made during the teaching.

I. Sacrament of Mercy

   A. We need this sacrament when our lives start to sink

   B. Jesus reaches out to save us like he reached out to St. Peter

II. Theological Foundation for the Sacrament

   A. God is love (1 John 4:8)

     1. God's very nature is love—he is a community of Persons in the Trinity

     2. When we turn away from God's love, he seeks us out

   B. God's revelation of himself in Exodus 34:6 is mercy and steadfast love

   C. *Hesed,* Hebrew for "committed love" or "sustained love"

Come unto me, antique illustration © Restored Traditions. All rights reserved.

    D. Jesus is constantly going out in his public ministry to seek others

    E. John 20:19–23

        1. Jesus sends his Apostles out with authority to forgive sins

        2. They continue the ministry of reconciliation started by Jesus

        3. John 20:23—**"If you forgive the sins of any they are forgiven."**

    F. Second Corinthians 5:18–20—Paul and the other Apostles share in this ministry

        1. This authority is passed on from the Apostles to their successors

        2. The priest behind the priest: Jesus

        3. The priest acts in the Person of Christ the Head

III. Why Can't I Just Go to God Directly?

    A. We're all called to go straight to God every day

    B. Confession is the most direct way to go to God for his forgiveness

    C. God has always worked through mediators (Moses, Elijah, Elisha, the Apostles)

IV. Why Does It Make Sense That God Set Up Confession This Way?

    A. It is very healthy to acknowledge mistakes and receive forgiveness

    B. God knows what we need

V. What Are the Effects of the Sacrament?

    A. We are reconciled with God (CCC 1468)

    B. We are reconciled with God's family, the Church (CCC 1469)

    C. We encounter the healing power of God's mercy

VI. Rite of Penance

    A. First step is to prepare ahead of time with an examination of conscience

    B. Confess our sins and sincerely try to remember all of them

    C. Penance is an expression of love after receiving the free gift of forgiveness

    D. Words of absolution—Jesus is present, and he is the one forgiving us of our sins

VII. Woman Caught in Adultery as an Image of Confession

    A. Jesus did not condemn her in her sin

    B. He loved her too much to leave her in her sin: "Go and sin no more."

SESSION 5 | ANSWERING COMMON QUESTIONS ABOUT CONFESSION

> "Forgiveness of sins brings reconciliation with God, but also with the Church."
> —CCC 1462

STEP 4: DISCUSS

Read the following questions, giving the small groups time to answer each one. Refer to the suggested answers in italics below each question as needed to help facilitate conversation. Answers will, of course, vary.

1. Matt had been away from Confession for seven years. He had been living far from God and came to a breaking point. Not knowing where to turn, he went to the parish and got in line for Confession. He writes about his experience: "When I heard the words of absolution from the priest, it was as if heavy chains fell away from my body. I experienced a sense of freedom and joy that I had never known. That was nearly twenty years ago, and today, I am still that changed man! How does Matt's story emphasize our psychological need and spiritual need of the sacrament?

(Our psychological and spiritual needs can be summarized with 3 C's: courage, conscience, and contrition. We have the need to be courageous and take responsibility for our actions. We also have the need to unburden our conscience when we make mistakes. And, finally, we have the need to express our remorse and ask for forgiveness for the mistakes we have made. Our effort in these areas is how we die to self and mature as Christians. The inability to practice reconciliation leaves us "stuck in a rut" and prevents our growth as an individual and in our relationships with others.)

2. In *The Fate of Empires and the Search for Survival,* historian Sir John Bagot Glubb (1897-1987) chronicles the decline and collapse of great empires and identifies a similar cycle in all. In the beginning, collective self-sacrifice and discipline builds the empire. Prosperity follows and leads to greater comfort, less religious practice, and moral decline. Finally, moral decline leads to selfishness, decadent living, and eventual collapse. How does this cycle demonstrate the corporate nature of sin and the need for the Sacrament of Reconciliation?

The adulteress by Lotto © Restored Traditions.
All rights reserved.

(The Catechism teaches: "The sinner wounds God's honor and love, his own human dignity as a man called to be a son of God, and the spiritual well-being of the Church, of which each Christian ought to be a living stone" [CCC 1487]. Our sin wounds the family of God and the Church's impact on society. This is why the priest is not only a representative of Jesus in the confessional, he is also a representative of the Christian community. Therefore, the effects of the sacrament are reconciliation with God and reconciliation with God's family, the Church.)

3. Jesus says to the woman caught in adultery: *"Neither do I condemn you; go, and do not sin again"* **[John 8:11]. His words demonstrate that God loves us just as we are but too much to leave us there! Why is it not enough to say that "God loves you just as you are?"**

(God loves us in our sin and imperfection. However, he loves us too much to leave us there. His goal is to prepare us for Heaven by changing us **"into his likeness from one degree of glory to another"** *[2 Corinthians 3:18]. This preparation for Heaven is the process of purifying us from all attachment to sin. It is serious work, one that requires both God's grace and our effort, because the more we are attached to sin the less we will desire Heaven. Author C.S. Lewis writes in the* Great Divorce: *"There are only two kinds of people in the end: those who say to God, "Thy will be done," and those to whom God says, in the end, 'Thy will be done.' All that are in Hell, choose it.")*

SESSION 5 | ANSWERING COMMON QUESTIONS ABOUT CONFESSION

STEP 5: COMMIT—*ENCOUNTERING GOD'S MERCY*

*Direct participants to the **COMMIT** section on page 49 of their Study Guides, and encourage them to spend time with this take-home assignment and be prepared to share the next time the group meets.*

The story of the prodigal son is perhaps one the most familiar of the many parables that Jesus tells. This narrative of sin, repentance, and forgiveness is a wonderful illustration of how we can encounter God in Confession. Read through this passage slowly and prayerfully:

> *"There was a man who had two sons; and the younger of them said to his father, 'Father, give me the share of property that falls to me.' And he divided his living between them. Not many days later, the younger son gathered all he had and took his journey into a far country, and there he squandered his property in loose living. And when he had spent everything, a great famine arose in that country, and he began to be in want. So he went and joined himself to one of the citizens of that country, who sent him into his fields to feed swine. And he would gladly have fed on the pods that the swine ate; and no one gave him anything. But when he came to himself he said, 'How many of my father's hired servants have bread enough and to spare, but I perish here with hunger! I will arise and go to my father, and I will say to him, 'Father, I have sinned against heaven and before you; I am no longer worthy to be called your son; treat me as one of your hired servants.' And he arose and came to his father. But while he was yet at a distance, his father saw him and had compassion, and ran and embraced him and kissed him. And the son said to him, 'Father, I have sinned against heaven and before you; I am no longer worthy to be called your son.' But the father said to his servants, 'Bring quickly the best robe, and put it on him; and put a ring on his hand, and shoes on his feet; and bring the fatted calf and kill it, and let us eat and make merry; for this my son was dead, and is alive again; he was lost, and is found.' And they began to make merry."*
>
> —Luke 15:11–24

Consider the younger son at the beginning of this parable. When he asks for his share of the inheritance, he is basically telling his father, "I prefer what you have to who you are—I want your stuff, but I don't want you anymore." How do you think this made the father feel?

Have the participants write their reflections in the space provided in the Study Guide.

When the son had squandered his inheritance, he quickly realized how empty his chosen lifestyle was. He wanted to go home, but he felt like his poor choices were in the way of returning to the way things were. How is this like (or unlike) our experience of sin?

Have the participants write their reflections in the space provided in the Study Guide.

The father must have been watching for his son because he saw him "while he was yet at a distance." This loving and compassionate father couldn't wait for his son to make it all the way home, so he ran to meet him. And he was so eager to forgive him and welcome him home that he didn't even let his son finish the apology he had planned out. It was enough that his son desired to come home. How do you think the son felt when his father welcomed him in this way? Have you had a similar experience in your life that you would be willing to share with us?

Have the participants write their reflections in the space provided in the Study Guide.

In the Sacrament of Reconciliation, Our Lord watches for us and runs to meet us. It is enough that we desire to come home. When we come to the sacrament with sorrow for our sins, God welcomes us home and wraps us in his grace. We were dead, and now we are alive again. We were lost, and now we are found.

Make an appointment with God to encounter his loving mercy in the Sacrament of Reconciliation. Find a time when you can go to Confession. Write it down. And begin preparing now and praying for the grace of a good confession.

The words Appointment written on a calendar © shutteratakan /shutterstock.com

SESSION 5 | ANSWERING COMMON QUESTIONS ABOUT CONFESSION

> "Come now, let us reason together, says the LORD: though your sins are like scarlet, they shall be as white as snow; though they are red like crimson, they shall become like wool."
>
> —Isaiah 1:18

STEP 6: WRAP-UP AND CLOSING PRAYER

Review the key points of this session together, and then end in prayer.

Here are the key points participants should take away from this session:

1. The Sacrament of Reconciliation flows out of God's nature of steadfast love and mercy.

2. We confess our sins to a priest because Jesus gave his Apostles the authority to continue his ministry of reconciliation and forgive sins.

3. Confession makes sense on a human psychological level because we all need to get things off our chest and have the peace of forgiveness.

4. In Confession we are reconciled to both God and the Church, and we receive God's healing mercy.

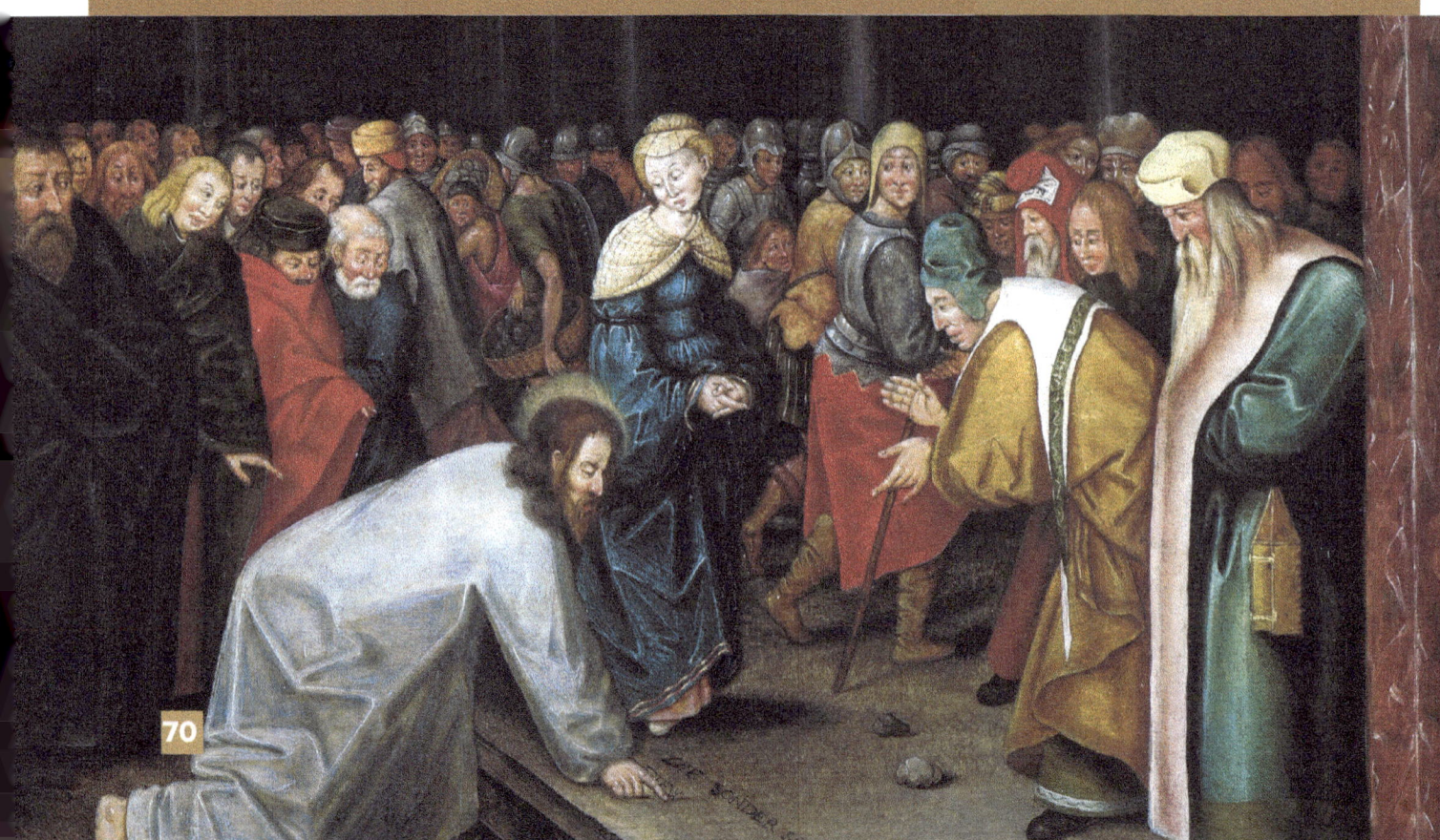

CLOSING PRAYER

To you, O Lord, I lift up my soul.
O my God, in you I trust, let me not be put to shame;
let not my enemies exult over me.

Make me to know your ways, O Lord; teach me your paths.
Lead me in your truth, and teach me, for you are the God of my salvation;
for you I wait all the day long.
Be mindful of your compassion, O Lord, and of your merciful love,
for they have been from of old.
Remember not the sins of my youth, or my transgressions;
according to your mercy remember me, for your goodness' sake, O Lord!
Good and upright is the Lord; therefore he instructs sinners in the way.
He leads the humble in what is right, and teaches the humble his way.
All the paths of the Lord are mercy and faithfulness,
for those who keep his covenant and his testimonies.
For your name's sake, O Lord, pardon my guilt, for it is great.

Turn to me and be gracious to me; for I am lonely and afflicted.
Relieve the troubles of my heart, and bring me out of my distresses.
Consider my affliction and my trouble, and forgive all my sins.

Amen.

—Psalm 25:1–2, 4–11, 16–18

FOR FURTHER STUDY

Catechism of the Catholic Church, 1420–1498

FREQUENTLY ASKED QUESTIONS ABOUT CONFESSION

A penitent goes to Confession, and then several hours later remembers that he forgot to confess a particular mortal sin. Is his Confession still valid? How does the penitent rectify the situation?

Yes, the penitent's Confession is valid, provided that at the time of confession he did not knowingly and willingly withhold confessing a mortal sin (e.g., out of shame). In this case, he has made a valid and fruitful Confession, and he can be confident that he is in the state of grace. However, he is to mention the forgotten mortal sin at his next Confession, in order "to complete the Sacrament" (Aquinas).

Similarly, a Catholic has been living a sacramental life and frequents Confession on a monthly basis. Then one day he remembers a mortal sin that he committed many years ago, and he is certain that he has never confessed this sin. Does this mean that he has not been living in the state of grace for all these years?

If this penitent has made a good examination of conscience before Confession and has not willingly withheld any sin from the confessor, then he or she can be at peace, and does not need to abstain from Holy Communion. However, the penitent should mention this sin in his next Confession because it completes the sacramental healing process, and also puts the soul at peace (there will be no more need to worry or think about this sin).

A penitent forgets the penance assigned by the priest. What should he or she do?

If the penitent is still within the confessional, it would be appropriate to ask the confessor to repeat the penance. If this does not happen, then the penitent can bring up this matter at the next Confession and ask the confessor to resolve the situation with his sacramental authority.

If a penitent's conscience accuses him of having committed a mortal sin, and yet he fails to mention this sin in Confession—out of fear or pride, for example—then he makes a sacrilegious and invalid Confession. Therefore, none of his mortal sins are forgiven, and he incurs an additional mortal sin of a sacrilegious Confession. At his next Confession, he must confess three things: the invalid Confession, the hidden mortal sin, and all the mortal sins he mentioned in the invalid Confession. Is there anything else he must do?

No, the penitent does not need to do anything more. In this case the confessor must be very compassionate and understanding, in order to allow the penitent to experience the joy of "coming home." The priest's gentle disposition also strengthens the penitent to avoid giving in to human respect at future confessions.

It's not about what it is.
It's about *Who* it is.

Prepare yourself and your parishioners to receive Jesus in the Eucharist as never before with *Presence: The Mystery of the Eucharist*. World-renowned Catholic presenters unveil the truth and beauty behind the "source and summit" of the Christian life, from its origins in Sacred Scripture, to its profound role in the life of the Church and its members.

Learn more at AugustineInstitute.org/Presence

Presence
THE MYSTERY OF THE EUCHARIST

AUGUSTINE INSTITUTE